KT-219-606

Fiona Sampson is a leading British poet and writer. Published in thirty-seven languages, she's received international awards in the US, India, Macedonia, Albania and Bosnia. A Fellow of the Royal Society of Literature, Fellow of the English Association and Fellow of the Wordsworth Trust, she's received an MBE from the Queen for Services to Literature, and published twenty-nine books. National prizes include the Newdigate Prize, Cholmondeley Prize, Hawthornden Fellowship, and various awards from the Arts Councils of England and of Wales, Society of Authors, Poetry Book Society and the Arts and Humanities Research Council. A former violinist, she is also a broadcaster and newspaper critic, and was editor of *Poetry Review* 2005-12. Her biography, *In Search of Mary Shelley* (2018), has been internationally critically acclaimed and was shortlisted for the Biographers' Club Slightly Foxed Prize. The poems in this book have received two major European prizes, the 2019 Naim Frashëri Laureateship of Albania and Macedonia, and the 2020 European Lyric Atlas Prize, Bosnia.

C016495603

Also by Fiona Sampson

Poetry:

The Catch
Coleshill
Night Fugue: New and selected poems
Rough Music
Common Prayer
The Distance Between Us
Travel Diary
Folding the Real
Picasso's Men

Non-fiction:

In Search of Mary Shelley
Limestone Country
Lyric Cousins
Beyond the Lyric
Percy Bysshe Shelley
Music Lessons
A Century of Poetry Review
Poetry Writing
On Listening
Writing: Self and Reflexivity (with Celia Hunt)
Creative Writing in Health and Social Care
A Fine Line (with Jean Boase-Beier & Alexandra Buchler)
The Healing Word
The Self on the Page (with Celia Hunt)

Translator:

Evening Brings Everything Back by Jaan Kaplinski
Day by Amir Or

COME DOWN

FIONA SAMPSON

corsair poetry

CORSAIR POETRY

First published in Great Britain in 2020 by Corsair Poetry

1 3 5 7 9 10 8 6 4 2

Copyright © 2020 by Fiona Sampson

The moral right of the author has been asserted.

All rights reserved.
No part of this publication may be reproduced, stored in
a retrieval system, or transmitted, in any form or by any means, without
the prior permission in writing of the publisher, nor be otherwise circulated
in any form of binding or cover other than that in which it is published
and without a similar condition including this condition
being imposed on the subsequent purchaser.

A CIP catalogue record for this book
is available from the British Library.

ISBN: 978-1-4721-5516-0

Printed and bound in Great Britain by
Clays Ltd, Elcograf S.p.A.

Papers used by Corsair are from well-managed forests
and other responsible sources.

MIX
Paper from
responsible sources
FSC® C104740

Corsair Poetry
An imprint of
Little, Brown Book Group
Carmelite House
50 Victoria Embankment
London EC4Y 0DZ

An Hachette UK Company
www.hachette.co.uk

www.littlebrown.co.uk

FOR MY FAMILIES

in illo tempore

Contents

Come Down

where a bridge
narrows
the fast-moving river
two movements
contrary and conjoined
when water
rushes against stone
that hands itself
like a passing shadow
over the bright
river surface
racing away
from the shock of self
come and see
stone moon down
like memory
through water cold enough
to drown you
two movements crossing
over cannot
pass but they do
while sky steps
continually out
of the river

*

Deaf

Are you listening you are
listening to the world
you think but you hear yourself
over and over the dark tongue

of world its hidden places
under trees beyond the lights
darkness falling from your feet
so deep you could fall through it

forever and how loud world
is with night in the trees
like a roost of galahs rising
the dark tongue of world

rising up through you as you
fall dear self dear
lonely self falling silently
mouthing through sound

Lady of the Sea

Blue and black
the Virgin sits
in her high
palanquin

she does not
regard us her
regard is drawn
back from us

far back
among the centuries
where she comes
from and where

she is going
already she is
travelling
past us and away

ancient star
flying so slowly
we do not
see her move

II

suppose she
compassionate
uncoiled her serpent's
arms or let

that black mask
fall could she
move among us
then or what

would be broken
and fired again
what understanding
newly perfected

III

high and far
very high
and far like
the disappearing

note of wind
shrilling between
glass comes
the tone the sweet

stone rings
when you knock
the saint's open
sarcophagus

IV

Lady in your
ark of rock
you who wear
the white stone

as a wedding
gown Lady
adamant
and personal

we carry you
in the eye's
reliquary
like a mote

or like a beam
that drowning we
could cling to —
Lady stronger

than time stronger than
light we see you
invisible
and everywhere

March Lapwings

Now everything
begins to move
and everything stays
where it is
each ash tree
and each hummock
shifts against
itself even
the grass shifts
and the electric
lapwings cry
change change
because the common
melts and flows
even the earth
flows like thawing
ice how lost
the senses are
in this disturbance
here it comes
again the new
electric cry
change change
as it moves past us

Frankenstein's Golem

Who is this
moving swiftly
through darkness
in a landscape
not yet given
form by daylight
slipping shapeless
as a shadow
through the dark
and unknown places
wearing night
next to his skin
wearing a pelt
of pine and stone
who is this
atoms seething
on his skin
who passes
through the dark
where he was buried
and from which
he was lifted
not by love
by power alone
lifted from death
and forced to pass

again through his own
dying who
slips away
between rocks (as
waterfalls
electrify
the dark) who is this
on the mountain
where mornings break
on the rocks
orange pink
terracotta
light new
and tenderly wrought?

Modern Prometheus

after Mary Shelley

he wakes / alone in the lab
to night noises / breath roaring like a machine
heart pistoning / life bumps in his chest
a live thing / in darkness
not yet separate from the dark / that dresses him
soothing his nakedness / with the uniform of authority
permitting everything / at least by daylight
he listens without realizing / is anybody there
hears rustling / a man alone with fear
doesn't want to be alone / wants to be alone
as night listens back / but something's changing
his mind / he squints
wrestling darkness / tries to understand
he wants to see / if knowledge is power
if sight lights the mind / if light salts the mind
his pupil stings / his iris winces
and what can he make out / understanding
only a little / and misunderstanding
a little more / the clockwork universe
like a dream / of knowledge

plunge then
into night
where you can imagine yourself
the first man
where you're nameless
and only you can see yourself
though you also don't
you want a good neighbour
the human dream
of belonging
some one to see yourself by
who am I
no answer comes
or silence is the answer
— sleep

till first sheep bells
wake him
and dawn reveals a man
he can't meet

throw yourself
into the unknown
a pioneer
unafraid
but soon to be famous
just as you want
you want to be known
to populate the dark
is anybody there
to make a companion
a mirror
asks a man alone
and time passes
that great denial
zero —

then tremoring test-tubes
snap him to attention
he recognizes
the one he turns away from

Wharf

When cattle stand on water
not afloat but pausing to graze
dark shining water they stand
gazing as if this were nothing

out of the ordinary having come
down an old slipway to graze
world turned upside down
by water where they alone

wait and will wait centuries
of beast insight come with them
to make a meal on the shiny
rim of darkness where clay

puggers heaved earth from itself
offering it up naked
and ready for the mould the patten
the kiln and the drying rack

Noumenon

Snow falls and fills a valley
and under its white roof
a sleeper dreams snow is falling
secretly for her alone
on and on in darkness
it falls like something speaking
noiselessly into silence

something that's all alone
in silence can't hear
itself can't feel grass or stones
or the small branches it conceals
even in the sleeper's dreams
falling snow cannot feel
the world it longs to touch

and misses falling through its own
cold embrace on and on
in the dark the sleeper dreams
snow is falling on her pillow
as wide wet words the night
speaks about itself snow
speaking the words for night

Boat Lane

I heard the South . . .
JOHN DAVIDSON

Down a lane
where bulrushes
taller than me
thrum   beetles
with antler claws

too heavy for them
stumble
at my feet
once again
and for the first time

I'm following
my father through
a salt stink
of fields the sea
can't forgive

for belonging
to it before
marsh rose up
soft soft
as shaking reeds

in sunlight
and someone built
a chalet among
the oaks down
along Boat Lane

I see the steep
shingle roof
between trees
where my grandparents
live time

without end
they watch me
following the lane
that leads towards
them and away

under pale
oak trees
whose branches
make a cage
filled with lights

and with the old
cries of doves
and where at night
owls flutter like rags
trapped

above the tideline
calling me
out of sleep
wild child
wild child

making shadows
leap the walls
of the steep
angled attic
among salt

sweet night
smells while out
across soughing
grass the sea
murmurs *loss*

and I float
from the open
night window
a scrappy moth
among the stars

that see themselves
reflected
and afloat
in infinite water
each one a coracle

adrift
in its own pool
but not like Moses
no I'm no
lost child

between the giant
yellow cress
and irises
cramming the waterways
with gaudy

as my father
walks ahead
into the glare
a violet streak
in the yellow

afternoon
and vanishes
while water pools
below a white
railing always

now and here
where the pillbox
entrance gapes
across the ditch
releasing

its toad stink
of piss and fear
remember round
the next bend
you can see

the Monument
and I do
with the window
wound right down
and a wide open

smell of France
blowing in
the car my father
Man of Kent
is following

the lane he's known
since he was
a child on Romney
before the war
and afternoon

is always green
and gold
between the reeds
where waders run
like ghosts of birds

as deep beneath
roots and silt
the boys who had
to ditch say their own
names mouthing

silently
the ones he
could not save
on missions over
the North Sea

but still the waves
lie and lie
the sea always
unsatisfied
breathing up

dykes and across
low fields
it condemns
the shabby pubs
and bungalows

while shadows pool
along Boat Lane
where my own
ghosts walk
on water Grandma

in flowered
housecoat Grandpa
carrying
his camera
here they come

down the lane
where bulrushes
taller than me
thrum   beetles
with antler claws

too heavy for them
stumble
at my feet
once again
and for the first time

I'm following
my father
who belongs
to marsh water
and to the sea

Cold War Afternoon

after Forough Farrokhzad

No not at all
the wind says
in the threshing
trees a south wind
glittering
among birch leaves
stirring up
the sycamore

once again
and long ago
the South Wind says
filling the garden
restlessly
with sunlight
as the roses
bend beneath it

lavish summer
promises
burn red
along their branches
till the wind
breaks petals
over itself
like a wedding

then ah the wind
says
as it fills
my arms and
empties
them remember
this remember
you who
are carried away
on the wind

The Nature of Gothic

What does it want
this cool stone
span this bridge
on air what
does it ask
of us who come
questioning
who move round
its feet our voices
licking at space
our desires make
currents stir
all up the air
that asks us to see
something
wonderful the roof
of the world
perhaps expects
some gravity
to open in us
reflection
or answer but
stone shifts
endlessly
into itself
it disappears

and reappears
like hours that slip
out of mind
then reappear
having been lost
to us while we
were lost among
the forest's pillars

Marsh

at Snape

We choose the room
we need to live in
each of us
imagining

the beams the walls
whitewash or stone
or maybe brick
the colour of fire

where RSJs
are simply steel
not metaphor
and the view

from wide
steel-framed windows
out of nineteen
seventy-nine

is ideal
and fair as it
frames the wild
salt reserves

where reeds stream
purple brown
into the wind
and water shakes

old terrors
loose *mutatis*
mutandis
you could take

this with you
your whole life
fragments of pitch
that might be birds

or voices
interrupted
how a grass
bank curves

diminishing
to those old people
doing Tai Chi
in the past

the way the marsh
rises and spreads
like echoes
into the sky

Line, Manticore

The line that is a creature
scratched in stone is
also a line of light
lipping along the mineral
edge of itself
light shining from stone
like flame from flint the lion
man shines and burns
in the holy stone
and blurred along the cut's
meniscus like tears
that absorb and spread
brightness its mineral
grain comes to light

II

Come touch the cut and feel
it open pale lips
that were spread already –
so topple between
change and nothing changing
that immense
blink of time in which
we are falling so slowly
we feel nothing the air
full of birdsong come
hold my hand so we
can fall hand in hand
together through the air
as we breathe it

Nothing much except
intention remains
of whoever scratched
a human beast into the wall
where the church
returns to itself
folding back a crucified
arm relinquishing
the gesture even as it
throws it wide across
the valley where
our hidden creature-
likeness   speaks   only
intermittently

IV

Wet stone smells
of lost meaning smells
of mysterious
wise intention
the unlived-in stonework
drawing back from us
as if it had been vowed
to a life apart
from us we can't witness
such austere design
being fallen altogether
into life together with
this large white
butterfly and so much sunlight

V

Small wonder warm
sun fills the stone
this is not the first
year nor the last
sunlight will return sliding
across a gutter skipping
the porch roof
to fill the thirsty stone
that changes colour
as heat gathers in it —
blood warm stone
drawing a trace of oil
from your finger when you
touch its cut face

VI

The line that is a creature
meets itself coming
the other way mane
back and tail appear
in turn then turn
back into a single
line scratching its way
again and endlessly
again through stone
to make this marriage contract
between man and beast
who are one flesh holy
and fallen

Carol

Words make a wavering
line in snow you follow them
though sometimes you can't see they'll
lead anywhere and often

they don't lead somewhere
but still you feel you must follow
hearing remembered voices
speaking   long ago

when you could not resist them
being lost in the drifting
world   you were a child
and voices sounded in the dark

far away and high above you
those giants whose rooms and gardens
are buried now in the snow dark

Vertigo

Suddenly
it isn't then
but now and this
familiar
wishful sound
the trees make
in wind is now
not then although
I still desire
the same things
the same way
their assurance
passes over
me there is
some other I
who sits in this
turbulent
sunlight and wishes
something that
she doesn't yet
know as freckles
fall onto her
shoulders from
the bridal leaves

Earthenware

To what green altar?

JOHN KEATS

The belly of this pot's
an earthbound O
that holds itself open
a space as if to practise
loving motherhood

or turns toward sun-
light through the window
on a June morning
still hazy with
the memory of rain

the way Earth turns
in science films
lifting first one side
then another out
of a deep blue

to face the sun how
we return to face
what we already saw
and seeing it retrace
our own remembered gestures

such a tender rite
it is that brings us home
to the light that vanishes
and returns
behind the wet roses

Mother as Eurydice

Suddenly I want to call
out to her
a slim girl (it seems)
(but she flickers)
to call her up

like a blue
flame
(she might blow out)
flickering in the doorway
of my first memory

she was beautiful
in ways impossible
to understand
not her bones face hair
or all of these

flickering because I was half-asleep
            because film judders
in the yellow doorway
of early memory
before the words come in

her gaze was
a blue
burning gasp
terrifying   perfect   gone

Walpurgis

This after sunset summer
light is the closest
we can come
to the strangeness of a white
night its borrowed time

in which trees stand
motionless they
go blind without the sun
and on the hill a deer
coughs again

exploratory
in the June night as bats
veer between power lines
while someone's radio
far downstream

might be illusion
as if sound misplaced
itself when everything
fell out of step
in the incomprehensible

bright dark and out
of the woods the festive
children could
come jiving and drumming
dressed for carnival

Stray

after Frances Cornford

All day the creek echoes among
stone and roots that the bridge
gathers and lets go currents
lumber and dead sheep jammed
any which way in the noise
of water you grow old and lonely
walker straying through a gate
and round a bend as you come
down among the rumours
into water's facetted gaze
for the creek has much to say
surrounding you with sounds you can't
decode oh fat pale woman in white
trainers whom nobody loves

Winterreise

Headlights move
slowly down
the hillside turn
this way and that
boxed-in by
invisible

hedges   look
how creature-wise
those lights work
from side to side
as if to solve
their problem

unhurried as
the predator
who drives with
a gun beside him
on the front seat
of his jeep

Old Man

Where were you then
in those desperate times
making me do the porno
moves while you watched
at home somewhere else
nothing was harming you
not loving did not
hurt it cost you nothing
closed hands and mouth
through our difference
I tried to touch you after
we fucked stroking your wide
back made you groan
with pleasure your eyes shut

Juno's Dream

Juno lies
under the earth
her great dreaming
has begun
and though she runs
on and on
through the turning
earth she will not
stir nor bring
the sheep home
nor catch the hare
she's dreaming of
as her bones make
a white sickle
as her skull
fills with the roots
of camomile
and willow as she
barks her mouth
full of the good
earth the smell
entering
and changing her
the dream turns
now she's running
towards us

running through
the earth that turns
towards us she
is almost home

Phenomenon

Snow falls and fills a valley
till the house fills with snow light
more clear more exact
than the usual musky daylight
where a little tenderness
waits like pencilled hatching
just to the side of things

that favourite chair or the crooked
table polished by dailiness
is laid bare   snow light
coming in from all sides looks
straight through the prism frankly
curious there is no myth
it says to equal this account

of surfaces and presences
it's an old story but we
live in it you and I
the snow light mentions as it comes
in making itself at home
among the chairs and the small
piles of books

Welcome

Love bade me welcome . . .

[   ]
       your whole-wheat grain
savoury
       as food for thought
redeems me
       time after time
when I break
       myself beside you

break myself
       into your no not
milk your
       comb-flecked honey
forgive me
       I'm still not finished
at your table

       even your impatience
says a grace
       to my daily bread
which you are
       warm on my tongue
flour-dust
       on my hands good
morning loaf

The Last Man

after Mary Shelley

Comes barefoot
over shining
turf over
clover and grass
each shiny stem
and leaf white
with frost is it
morning it is
the first morning
            comes walking
barefoot on grass
that bends and bends
under his feet
this is the rhythm
of prayer this
is how we always
knew it would be
bare feet in the bare
orchard
feet in ginnels
of the grass
            is this how
it will be walking
through the frost

under bare trees
when you are alone?

Manoeuvres

The European Union is the world's most successful invention for advancing peace.

JOHN BRUTON

A clear sky
and in your eye's
vitreous humour
two warplanes skid
like floaters

following a valley
through farmland they are
not defending
valleys and fields fat
on fair weather

good luck stacked
and baled
right to the river-
brink that shivers back
this dream —

reversed
cattle and pasture shake
and old patterns
fragment through water
where a skimmed stone

skipping the surface
to bruise that dark polish
leaves you
empty handed
arm lifted

in strange salute
for the suddenly
empty valley
the sky the long
shadows behind you

Wild Equinox

I

These days are still
cold the line of feeling
working its way thinly
up so we might touch
a pulse almost to life
or make the heart inside
an egg echo itself or
hear ants underfoot
raising their secret cities

II

Could we build
slow
slow from these

splinters
these frayed grains
strangely consorting

nails wire
tarpaulin
that seem to fit

is this the way
frail   shaking
at our touch

a barn begins?

III

What you pray for
hardly seems
to matter when
the valley holds
light with such
care any
way is it
so fragile this —
truth is it
or something like —

here but also
somehow not
it waits behind
all this for
its turn to speak
through each tree
and fencepost —
and since you're here
also to speak
through you

IV

Light outlines
these early buds

as if they were
bitten with

a burin as if
nitric acid

over-wrote
the speaking

tongues
of morning things

There are still
verticals
and the trees
clamber uphill
again this morning
to labour is
to pray even
when the clenched buds
of the pear tree
cannot help
themselves the valley
plunges on
miming *dawn* —
Confucians say
observance is
all there is —
and when we show
our hands are empty
something seems
to disappear some
light be lost
between the trees

VI

Dry season
in the heart
you have to pray
although you can't

but still the valves
of the magnolia
wrench
themselves upward

VII

Light speaks itself
along branches
flagged with Lenten white
symbol of origin
or of surrender

everything to come
hides its face
among the shaking tongues
of a tulip tree
we're dazzled

dumb   our faces burn
and still we send
the small creatures on
ahead of us
into the fire

VIII

How tenderly
familiar
tree bark is

suddenly
close like a new
truth:
the way witness

standing gravely
in light
lets itself
be seen and sees
in return

Unignorably
the ghost tree pours
upward raising
and raising itself
wild ducks fly
downstream

with lifted voices
and the white
flowers crowd
out of branches
that are holding
dark air up

everything is
and knows it is —
wild equinox
balancing light
with the
inseparable dark

At Last the Rye

Here we are walking
in moonlight through fields
of rye we pass through
their pale sea in
the summer night three
of us walking between
the bent heads the feathered
napes of holy rye
where we pass the field
opens the moon silvers
the path ahead of us
three of us walking one
will carry on and carry
on long after two
have called their dogs home
one will walk a strait
path through the silver
fields that do not end

COME DOWN

FOR MY IMMIGRANT ANCESTORS

I wanted to know the true nature of
the 'otherness' I had been born into,

SIDNEY NOLAN

Come down where it
narrows down
over the last field
where the valley squeezes
almost shut

then opens
come down
into light and dark
systole and diastole
water moving shadows

below beeches
and steep fields
come and find the place
you thought you remembered
not hidden

among trees but standing
at the valley corner
still the same a tall plain
house though you can't greet
the strangers

who crowd through it
they pass in and out
mouths moving silently
as if underwater
you can't read their lips

but light breaks
on the upturned faces
come down
as everything breaks off
mid-story   tractor tracks

a bucket at a gate
traces of the ones who left
just this morning
centuries ago
and is it here

in holy pantomime
that suddenly a horse
rears and rears all soundless
flash and buckle
and the dragon impaled

on the saint's spear
rears back
from hooves thundering
in silence by its head
one struggle knotted

in one stone where the red
stain spreads like something
entering a wound
to turn the blood that gallops
in your ears

or are those hooves
beyond the river
almost out of sight
among grey branches
tasselled gold

with mistletoe
is it rumour
or does something
watch you with terrified
beast eyes

it doesn't matter
sit down
take off your boots
and wash your feet in this
slow red river

where plastic sacks float
slide settle
as some ancient muscle
of sediment
breaks surface

like the backs
of giant lizards
that came down to drink
flexing their wings
time was already

calling them
and the small
white clouds
raced overhead
but you were neither

here nor anywhere
the valley didn't
know you yet
although you've always
known the light lying

along the top field
and the pear tree's
hieroglyph
because you stand just
out of frame

watching as if
from some shore
where once upon a time
and again
you witness say

a ship   lift
perhaps and come down
as a haar flagged with gulls
slips up its mast
carrying old smells

amid the ragged light
and bird-screams
of memory before
words this is not
desire as out

on the difficult water
a stranger sails away
with you into the future
where you and he
never meet

not even in the unknown
country that long
loneliness
where he's taking you who
don't speak his language

but this is what
it means to witness
this too is belonging
catching cold
while the youth on board

the distant ship
dreams of a child
who floats her face pale
her hair spread and tangled
like the dream

in which she hears
blood surf roar
far away beneath the world
and all night long
digs in sand believing she

can reach Australia
down and down she digs
and suddenly here
is wide scrubland
red rock the colour of home

and she is you
and you see wavering
like tears on the brim
of sight slowly appear
three children

walking an enormity
alone together
where the bare sky
meets the road
and this too is belonging

three lost children
taking the measure
of their strangeness
as the curious creatures
move past like

a doxology
and time folds
into another century
where you come walking
down with them

into the future
they won't arrive at
stay with them
in the plank house among roses
where they do arrive

at last and give thanks
in plain hymns in
the old tongue
as the evening river slides
past shining

come back
to the creek
you've never seen
step down
into light and darkness

water standing orange
pink terracotta
in the leads
wooden shacks
and a tin veranda

where you walk up to the bar
remembering
you were always here
in the body's
forethought in its heft

heat and juice
in the smile
of a stranger
who will never
speak your name

waiting with the mother
tongue to become local
like sandstone softening
as water threads
below beeches

and fields
that don't change
or change absolutely
depending who
comes down the slope

among faint
constellations
of wild plum
not ancestors but first comers
stumbling down

who believed in
the valley knowing already
its sly light
between leaves
lichen and hanging damp

smells as old
as another country
this too is belonging
where a blackbird calls
between the trees

so clearly now
or was it years ago
when you were a child
on a rope swing
still strange

figures pass you moving
through the orchard
as a breeze stirs
breathing seems
to fill the leaves and look

the old ones
keep passing through us
saying world is wide
we must come down
together into its valley

Surfacing

At last you climb
out of the dream
as if from
a dark valley
into light
letting all that was
uncertain come
clear on that high
pasture as each
preconception
melts in day-
light like shadows
do streaming
away under
the ragged thorns

was it this
woke you made you
clamber out
of yourself

little bare
creature   from your
sleeping self?

Acknowledgements

My grateful thanks to Bristol Festival of Ideas for commissioning 'Frankenstein's Golem', to the Royal Society of Literature for commissioning 'Manouevres' as part of their Peace Poems project, to the Keats-Shelley Memorial Association for commissioning 'Earthenware' for their celebration of the Keats Odes, and to the Aldeburgh Festival for commissioning 'Marsh'. 'Boat Lane' was also premiered at the Aldeburgh Festival. 'Modern Prometheus' was commissioned for Maya Attoun's 'The Charms of Frankenstein' at the Jewish Museum, London.

Acknowledgements are due to the editors of the following publications for permission to reprint some of these poems: *FT, Irish Times, New Statesman, Spectator, Poetry London, Spears, London Magazine, Next Review, Temenos, Resurgence, Axon, The Kindling, The Border* (ed. Amy Wack, Seren, 2018).

Some of these poems have been published in translation in: *Tema* (Zagreb), *Terras* (Rotterdam), *Poesis International* (Bucharest), *Kefel*, *Pema e Hijes* (Tetova). An earlier version of this collection appeared in Romanian translation by Diana Manole as *Întoarce-te* (Tracus Arte, Bucharest).

I am grateful to Archipelago Publishing House, Dajana Dedovic and the Museum of Language and Letters for a residency at Tršić, Serbia, which enabled work on this collection.

Most of all, for their support I would like to thank Sarah Castleton and Olivia Hutchings at Corsair, my agent Sarah Chalfont and, always, Peter Salmon.